CURTISS P-40

in action

by Ernest R. McDowell

illustrated by Don Greer

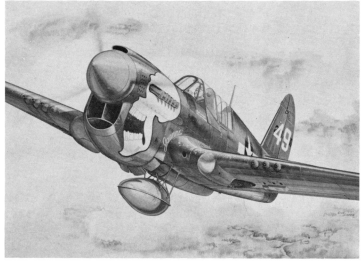

[Cover] Shown banking over the jungles of Burma is this P-40N-5-CU of the 89th Fighter Squadron, 80th Fighter Group based at Karachi, India in 1943. The plane is basically overall Olive Drab 41, Medium Grey under surfaces.

 squadron/signal publications

ISBN 0-89747-025-7

If you have any photographs of the aircraft, armor, soldiers or ships of any nation, particularly wartime snapshots, why not share them with us and help make Squadron/Signal's books all the more interesting and complete in the future. Any photograph sent to us will be copied and the original returned. The donor will be fully credited for any photos used. Please send them to: Squadron/Signal Publications, Inc., 1115 Crowley Dr., Carrollton, TX 75011-5010.

To Mary, Donald, and Betsy

Photo Credits

USAF Museum
Mr. Casey, Smithsonian Institution
USAF Magazine & Book Branch
AAHS
IPMS
Curtiss-Wright Corp.
William J. Balogh, Sr.
Col. R.L. Baseler USAF
Gerry Beauchamp
Steve Birdsall
Maj. J.W. Boyce USAF
Lionel Bruce
Dale Caldwell
Fred C. Dickey, Jr.
Royal Frey
Garry L. Fry
James P. Gallagher
Robert Gebhardt
Richard M. Hill

Dr. Richards H. Hoffman
Robert C. Jones
Michel Lavigne
Malcolm Long
MSgt. David W. Menard USAF
Eric Nicolle
Col. Joel B. Paris USAF
Geoff Pentland
Kel Perks
Earl Reinert
Kenn C. Rust
MSgt. Norman Taylor USAF
Manosuke Toda
Richard Ward
David Weatherill
Phil Yant
G.J. Zwanenburg

Night firing test of the six .50 caliber machine guns mounted on the P-40E. Time exposure shows the cone of fire obtained when fired from a semi-stationary position. Subject to vibration the pattern would have been larger in aerial firing. [USAF Museum]

P-40
Development

Few aircraft designs have had as odd or complex a background as the P-40 series. In fact one wonders why the Air Corps elected to give the H-75P a designation other than a dash number in the P-36 series since it was basically a re-engined P-36A. Spin-offs from the P-36 design would result not only in the P-40 but the XP-37, XP-42, XP-46, XP-53, XP-60, and XP-62 plus the ones given Y designations and various dash numbers.

Ignoring the Curtiss Hawk biplanes, the family tree of the P-40 would seem to have its tap roots in the XP-934 Curtiss **Swift** of 1932 vintage. Although some experience in the low-wing monoplane type was gained when the company produced its famed **Shrike** series of attack planes, the **Swift,** or XP-31 as it was designated by the Air Corps, was their first low-wing pursuit design. By one of those odd quirks, the **Swift** initially was powered by an in-line engine which gave way to a more powerful radial, just the reverse of the P-36 to P-40 design development. The XP-31 was not successful with either engine and the design was soon abandoned (It did earn the dubious distinction of being the last U.S. pursuit plane with a fixed landing gear). The Curtiss Company's fortunes took a downward turn in the pursuit field when the Boeing P-26A was selected by the Air Corps over the XP-31.

Working for Northrop, a certain Donovan R. Berlin failed to see eye-to-eye with management and was asked to leave. Having previously been with Douglas and prior to that with McCook Field, his qualifications were ideal for a design project that Ralph Damon, the head of Curtiss, had in mind. He was

P-36A in RAF battle camouflage in England early in the war. As this was the sire of the P-40 series the family resemblances abound. An agile but lightly armed pursuit, the P-36A was likened to a thoroughbred race horse when compared with the early model of the P-40 which was described as not unlike a dray horse. [Royal Frey]

The XP-40 Prototype, Air Corps serial number A.C. 38-10. Designer Donovan R. Berlin elected to locate the scoop for the radiator under the belly, but fear that it might be damaged by debris thrown up by the slipstream on takeoff and landing led to its relocation. Berlin was later proven correct when the North American P-51 flew with the radiator in the same location. [USAAF]

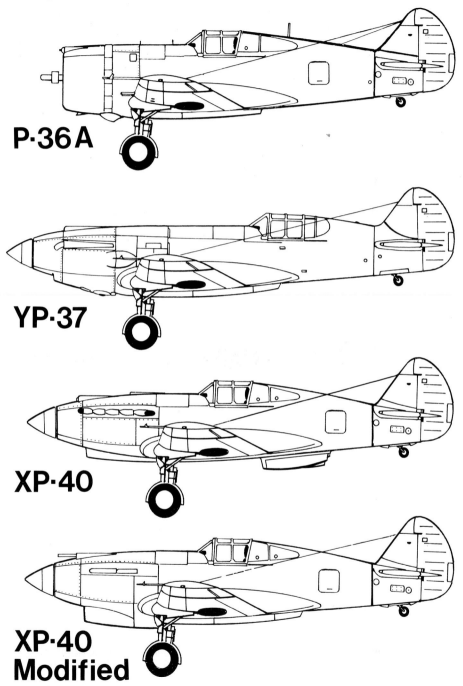

P-36A

YP-37

XP-40

XP-40 Modified

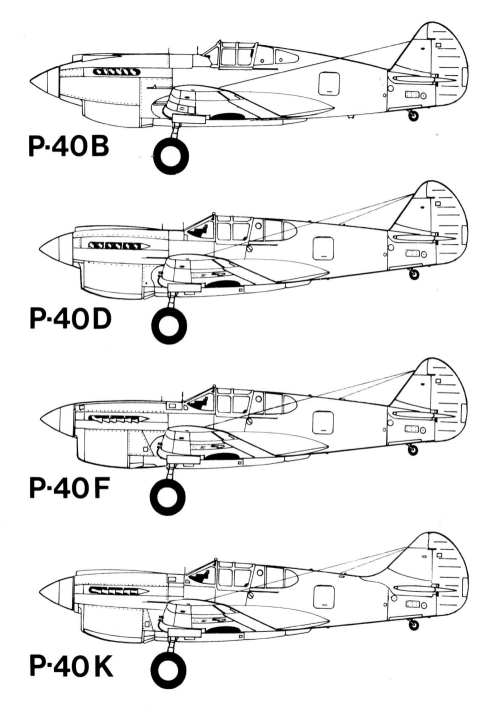

P-40B

P-40D

P-40F

P-40K

hired and made project engineer on design number 75. Berlin was advised that he would be expected to have a model ready to test within seven months and that it would be expected to win an Army Air Corps contract. Armed with the Air Corps performance specifications, he plunged into the project with a will. The project was completed on schedule, the first flight being made in April, 1935. The anticipated competition for an Army contract was postponed several times before DeSeversky finally was declared the winner and awarded the contract. Curtiss, however, was given a contract for three service test airplanes to be known as the Y1P-36. This model was entered in the competition the following year and won it. An order for 210 aircraft followed on June 6, 1937 plus another order from France for 200 more.

Despite the fact that the design was a fine one, it was becoming more obvious by the day that it would soon be outclassed by foreign designs. Having no desire to fall behind again, work was commenced on a new design that was hoped would be developed into a 300 mph plus pursuit ship. The proposal was to drastically rework the standard P-36 fuselage, incorporate the Allison chemically-cooled engine, and a turbo supercharger. A projection of the expected performances was enough to cause the Air Corps to order a test airplane under the designation of XP-37. When Hawk Model 75-I was finished it looked more like a racing plane than a fighting aircraft. It looked fast. It proved to be just that in the air as it became the first American pursuit plane to exceed 300 mph. The big Allison V-1710-11 engine which was rated at 1,000 horsepower at 20,000 feet was balky but the XP-37 achieved the promised 340 mph speed in tests. The cockpit had been moved far aft to overcome a center of gravity problem and to provide space for the turbo-intercooler and, radiator, both of which were mounted forward of the pilot's compartment; as a result, the pilot's vision was restricted and poor. Further, it was found that the supercharger simply was not far enough along in its own development to be reliable. Despite these obvious short-comings the Air Corps ordered 13 service test aircraft as YP-37s. Some modifications were made to improve the XP-37 but the resulting aircraft had an even longer nose. Because of this, together with recurrent supercharger problems, the YP-37 model was dropped.

Don Berlin suggested that a P-36A airframe be mated with an Allison V-1710 modified to increase the diffuser rpms and produce 1,050 horsepower at 10,000 feet. As wind tunnel tests gave evidence that the design could be expected to attain about 350 mph at the rated altitude, a proposal was submitted to the Material Division at Wright Field on March 3, 1938. Impressed by the figures, the Air Corps issued A.C Contract 10136 to Curtiss on July 30, 1938 permitting Curtiss to use the tenth production airframe of the P-36A to test the idea under the designation XP-40, and to be delivered in February of 1939. Serial number A.C. 38-10 was assigned to the Test aircraft.

Producing the new airplane was more than just taking an airframe off the production line, bolting the Allison to it, and bending some sheet metal to enclose the nose and engine. Problems with weight and balance had to be worked out and a new center of gravity determined. The liquid cooled engine required many items not needed on a radial engined airplane. These items had to be designed to fit into a rather small nose cross-section, be placed to gain the maximum efficiency and still be easy to reach when it came to maintenance. Coolant tanks, coolant radiators, oil radiator, the assorted plumbing that these new items required as well as air intakes, gun mounts etc. all had to be woven into the design. Finished, it stood on the flight line, its gleaming natural finish shining like a jewel.

Like the XP-37, it looked fast when compared to the more compact and stubby looking P-36A. What caught the eye was the long pointed nose. As the gaze swept aft it took in the coolant radiator which had been placed on the ventral centerline of the fuselage just behind the wings trailing edge, a position that would later be used on the North American P-51, but one that would be changed on the XP-40. The oil cooler, circular in shape, was located on the underside of the nose cowling and neatly faired into the centerline. An air intake for the carburetor was located on the nose just forward of the windshield. Fairing plates were fitted to the landing gear to provide an in flight seal when the gear was in the retracted position. This practice had been carried over from the P-36A model. Large fairings were provided where the wing joined the fuselage. Twin machine gun mountings were located over the engine and the barrels were protected by more fairings. Small vertical slit exhaust panels were used to provide progressive exhausting to relieve the heat and pressure on the aft end of the manifold which terminated in an large flared exit.

The prototype made its maiden flight on October 14, 1938 with Edward Elliott, the assistant chief test pilot, at the controls. The XP-40 seemed to be a success but a few modifications were made including moving the ventral radiator forward to a nose position. A fighter competition was held in January of 1939 and the XP-40 had no trouble beating out the XP-37, XP-38, XP-39, AP-4, and Hawk 75-R. Curtiss was awarded Air Corps Contract No. 12414 on April 26, 1939 for 524 P-40s at a cost of $12,872,898.00.

Continued testing brought out the fact that the XP-40 was not living up to performance expectations. Speed-wise the best that could be obtained from the plane was about 340 mph. Although some modifications had been made in December 1938, the speed was not helped. The modifications included blast tubes for the machine guns which had been mounted. Air for the carburetor was now being drawn in through the oversized gun fairing. The two ducts merged at a point further back over the engine and fed air to the down-draft carburetor located on the rear face of the engine. This arrangement removed the air scoop box from the top of the cowling. The coolant radiator had been moved forward and located under the nose in a chin type arrangment. A two pipe exhaust system was fitted which retained the flared rear outlet and increased the engines performance by a small increment. A blister was added to the leading edge of each wing, its purpose was to eliminate any tail buffeting and delay stalling by about four degrees. These modifications improved general performance but the XP-40 still did not meet the Air Corps requirements nor even the Curtiss performance guarantee of 360 mph top speed. With added wind tunnel testing at N.A.C.A., Langley Field, Virginia based on another series of modifications indicating that the desired results could be achieved, the Air Corps implemented the contract. The H-75P or XP-40 was returned to the Buffalo Plant where an improved Allison V-1710-33 (C-15) engine was fitted along with a larger radiator scoop. In December of 1939 after all of the modifications had been made the XP-40 reached a top speed of 366 mph at the specified 15,000 foot altitude. It was now ready to go into mass production.

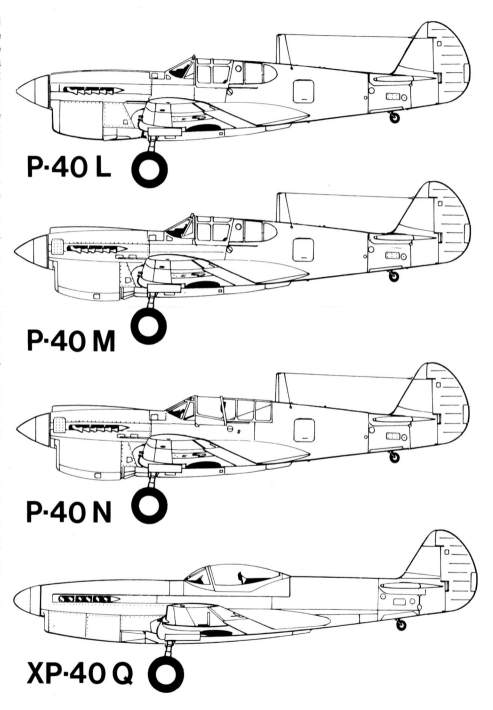

P-40 L

P-40 M

P-40 N

XP-40 Q

The XP-40 Prototype in final form, now carrying twin .50 cal. machine guns in oversized blast tubes, which doubled as caburetor intakes. The most obvious external alteration is the repositioning of the radiator air scoop.

Nose Armament Development

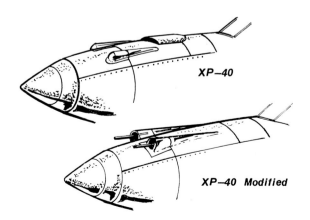

XP-40

XP-40 Modified

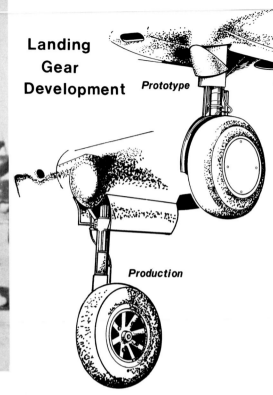

Landing Gear Development

Prototype

Production

P-40s of the 31st Pursuit Group at Selfridge Field, Michigan in late 1940. Traces remain of the aircraft number under the exhaust stubs as well as in the more normal position on the fin. [John Hulme]

Bearing an unusual roundel, a P-40 of the 20th Pursuit Group's 79th Squadron at Paine Field, Washington is getting an early morning pre-flight check. [Fred C. Dickey]

The sleek lines of the Tomahawk are emphasized by this frontal shot. The aircraft was a clean one. Note the once again relocated carburetor intake. [USAF Museum]

P-40-P-40C Tomahawks

Curtiss redesignated the production model the H-81 and went into production in March of 1940. Flush riveting was introduced on the production aircraft to further reduce drag. Armament consisted of two .50 caliber machine guns mounted in the nose plus a single .30 caliber gun in each wing. The line turned out eleven aircraft in March but three were set aside for service trials as there had been no provision made for any YP-40s. The first model off the line, A.C. serial number 39-156, was put through a series of tests that established its top speed at 357 mph at 15,000 feet, a service ceiling of 32,750 feet, a rate of climb of 3,080 feet during the first minute and it took 5.3 minutes to reach 15,000 feet. Cruising speed was about 277 mph and it landed at 80 mph.

Changes made to the aircraft during the production run included a redesigned landing gear in which the fairings were eliminated, two small doors were added and located on either side of the strut recess, closing to seal the strut portion of the undercarriage while a smooth wheel plate effectively covered the wheel recess during flight. Short curved exhaust stacks replaced the manifold exhaust. The carburetor air intake was relocated just behind the propeller spinner and connected to the carburetor by a long ducting running aft and down. The oil and coolant radiators were redesigned and clustered together with the one oil and two Prestone radiators forming a triangle. The machine gun blast tubes were modified and reduced in size. An additional .30 caliber machine gun was mounted in each wing. The fuel system was revised.

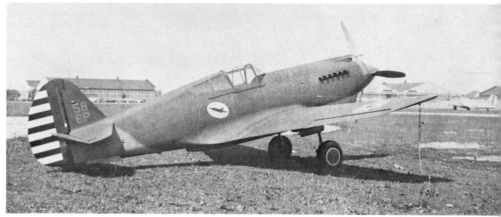

After accepting delivery of the first 200 P-40s, the USAAC deferred the remaining 324 to allow Curtiss to fill a French contract for 140 desperately needed H-81A's. Despite this action, these aircraft were not to reach France before that nation collapsed. The almost equally desperate British took over the French contract for the RAF. Arriving in the UK many of this batch still had French instrumentation and lacked armor plating, self-sealing tanks, and

P-40s of the three Squadrons of the 8th Pursuit Group pre-war. [Top] A P-40 of the 33rd Fighter Squadron probably taken at Mitchell Field, NY showing the squadron insignia of an eagle's claw. [Balogh-Menard] [Center] P-40 of the 8th Pursuit Group's 35th Pursuit Squadron early in 1941 at Selfridge Field. Insignia is a leaping black panther. [Dickey] [Bottom] P-40 of the 36th Pursuit Squadron belonging to the Squadron Commander as denoted by the two fuselage bands. Insignia is laughing native wearing goggles. [USAF] Pre-war US markings were Olive Drab upper surfaces with Neutral Grey underneath. Tail was marked with Gloss Blue vertical stripe and alternating horizontal bands of Red and White. The spinner color denoted squadron within the Group; Red, Yellow and Blue being the most frequent colors, and most often being used in that order, as was the case with the 8th Pursuit Group. Numbering on the fin was in Insignia Yellow [on rare occasions Black], the numbers 1-39 being used for the Group's first Squadron, 40-79 for the second and 80-119 for the third.

P·40B

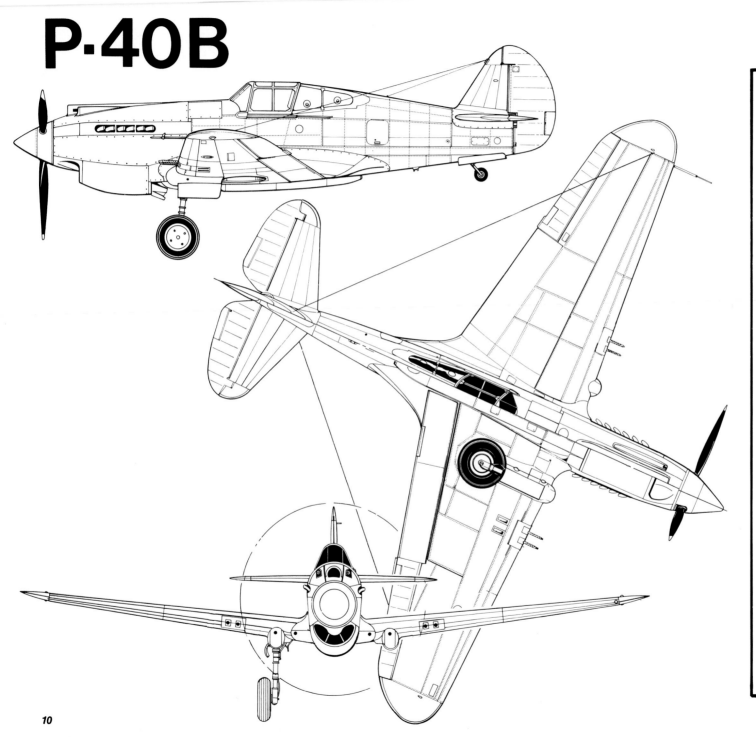

Number of Airplanes	131
Type Supercharger	Engine-driven Single stage blower
Dimensions:	
Length	31'8 9/ 16"
Height	12'4 1/4"
Tread	8' 2 1/8"
Landing Angle	13° 10'
Span	37' 3 1/2"
Weight & Balance:	
Design Gross Wght.	7352
Gross Wght.	7632
Weight Empty	5615
Engine:	
Manufacturer	Allison
Model	V-1710-C15
Army Designation	V-1710-33
Spec. Numbers	126-D
Take Off Rating	HP1100
Take Off Rating	RPM 2950-5 min.
Normal Rating	
HP	960
RPM	2600
Alt.	15,000
Military Rating	
HP	1090
RPM	3000
Alt.	15,000
Propeller:	
Manufacturer	Curtiss
Type	Electric
Diameter	11'0"
Min. Ground Clearance	8"
Fuel System:	
No. Fuel Tanks	3
Capacity:	
Normal	120
Maximum	158.5
Armament:	
Wing Guns - No., Caliber	4 (Fast fire) .30
No. Rounds per Gun	500 Inb'd gun 480 Outb'd gun
Gun Sight:	
Location	Bet. Pedals on Cl of Fus. & Below Inst. Board Supp. Tube
Gun Camera:	
Type & Location	None, None
Wing Bombs:	
Quantity & Size	None
Landing Gear:	
Main Ldg. Tire Type	30" S.C. 8 Ply
Brake Size	12 x 3 1/4
Radio:	
Type & Antenna Type	SCR-283 VEE
Battery:	
Type & Location	G-1, Fuselage

bullet proof windshields. The British mounted four Brownings in the wings and advised Curtiss of the changes desired so that later batches arrived with most of the RAF refinements already fitted. The RAF called the plane the Tomahawk I assigning serial number AH741 to the first one accepted and progressing through and including AH880 as the remainder arrived. Most of those retained in the UK were used as trainers or in an Army Cooperation role (close support). Many were shipped on to the RAF fighting the Axis in North Africa where they made their presence felt very quickly. They also proved to be tricky for the RAF pilots who were used to three point landings with the Spitfire. This was definitely not the way to bring in a Tomahawk unless one desired to execute a ground loop. They learned to bring her down with power on, touching the wheels down while holding the tail high, and then allowing her to settle on her own as she slowed in the roll out.

Some sources state that the "A" designation was never used. Others insist that it consisted of a single specimen which was intended as a reconnaissance airplane but simply did not work out. Another source believes that it was to have been the standard production version but that due to the many changes prior to production requested by the Air Corps or made by Curtiss they simply skipped over the P-40A designation for the sake of simplicity. It seems most likely that Curtiss did not produce any P-40A models at all and for all practical purposes it can be ignored.

Model H-81A-2 featured a number of refinements over the original P-40. All the changes introduced during the P-40 production run were retained, with the addition of such niceties as pilot armor, self-sealing tanks and an armored windscreen. New on most P-40Bs were underwing bomb shackles. The net result of all of these changes was a loss of performance because of the added weight. An order for 110 was placed by the RAF while the USAAC procured 131 to complete the balance of the original order that had been deferred in favor of the French. RAF serials ran from AH881 through AH990 inclusive. Air Corps serials were 41-5205 through 41-5304 plus 41-12397 through 41-13327 both inclusive.

The H-81A-3 was almost identical to the H-81A-2. Yet another new fuel system was installed to add additional 134 gallons to the fuel load, increasing the combat radius. Provisions were made to attach a 52 gallon drop tank below the fuselage center line. The SCR-283 radio was replaced by an SCR-24 7N type. The Air Corps ordered 193 of the P-40C models while the RAF purchased 930. Air Corps serials were 41-13328 through 41-13520 and RAF numbers ran through several blocks, AH991 to AH999, AK100 to AK570. From the British batches 100 were supplied to China and another 195 were turned over to the Russian Air Force. This model was the first of the series to engage in extensive combat operations.

The RAF, as was their custom removed the .30 calibers in favor of their own .303 caliber machine guns to simplify supply problems. Later a small number of RAF Tomahawks were given to Turkey. Undoubtedly the most famous batch was the one that eventually equipped the American Volunteer Group in China. The A.V.G. insured the P-40 a permanent niche in the aviation fighter aircraft hall of fame as the famed Flying Tigers wrote their own unequalled chapter in the history of aerial warfare. To paraphrase Sir Winston, "Never had so few done so much with so little". The C model was flown by pilots of at least eight different nations during its combat operational life.

Flight of Tomahawk Mark Is of no. 403 Squadron RCAF at Bagington in April, 1941.

RAF Tomahawk Mark I of the 1683 Bomber Defense Training Flight at Bruntingthorpe, U.K. coded FR-G and serial AH873. This aircraft was later assigned to Market Harborough in 1943. This flight staged mock attacks on bombers to give crews practice at leading and tracking fighters. Standard ETO day fighter finish of 1943-44 period with a six inch Yellow band along the leading edge of the wings. Spinner, fuselage band and code were all Sky. [R.C. Jones]

This P-40 was presented to the British; the inscription in the large roundel on the rear fuselage reads, "A Plane Gift - Real American Friendship [with those three words placed in descending order so that their initials read RAF] Builders of Camp Edwards, USA". [Balough-Menard]

[Above Left] Tomahawk Mark I RAF of F/L Henderson of no. 250 Squadron, no. 239 Wing in Western Desert 1942. [R.C. Jones] [Above] Kicking up the usual dust storm a Tomahawk of 4 Squadron SAAF in the foreground joins a Kittyhawk in the background from 2 Squadron as another Kittyhawk pilot of 2 Squadron sits in his cockpit on alert. [South African War Museum]

[Left] Major J.E. "Jack" Frost poses under the SAAF ensign in typical Western Desert attire of a P-40 squadron. [South African War Museum] [Below] Tomahawk Mark I of no. 4 Squadron SAAF at Gambut in 1942 sported this unit badge. Shield was Red, White and Blue with Gold code letters, Squadron motto "We've Had You" was Black on Gold, animal was several shades of Brown and Tan. [Lionel Bruce]

Nose Armament Development

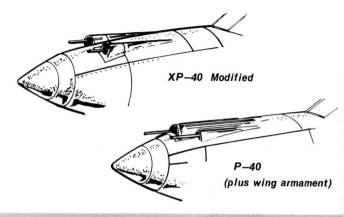

XP–40 Modified

P–40
(plus wing armament)

P-40Cs on the flight line at Chanute Army Air Field, Illinois early in 1942. The belly tanks were the easiest way to distinguish the P-40C from the B and P-40 models.

[Above Left] One of the pilots of No. 4 Squadron SAAF at landing Ground number 22, Egypt 1942 used a skeleton with a scythe on a rounded triangular background as his personal insignia on his P-40B.

A No. 4 Squadron Tomahawk in a not uncommon position at Amerjai in 1941. A new fin and rudder plus an entire wing section may have enabled this bird to fly again but on the whole it looks like a write off as the RAF was apt to put it. [Lionel Bruce]

SHARK MOUTH

While there have been aircraft on which a shark mouth was painted as far back as World War I, the motif attained its fame in the US as a result of the fame of the AVG (American Volunteer Group). Formed in 1941 under the leadership of Claire Chennault, the AVG became popularly known as the "Flying Tigers." Flying various marks of the P-40, the AVG wrote a chapter in aerial warfare that has yet to be surpassed. Using the 180 P-40C's lend-leased to China in early 1941, the Tigers were all experienced American pilots, flying for the Chinese Air Force. In the slightly more than nine months of its existence the AVG amassed a total of 286 confirmed kills of Japanese aircraft against only four combat losses. In July, 1942, the AVG was absorbed into the USAAF and renamed the 23rd Fighter Group. It remained in China throughout the war, eventually becoming part of the 1st Chinese-American Composite Wing.

However, the World War II usage of the sharkmouth did not originate with the AVG. Credit must be given to RAF No. 112 Squadron flying in the Western Desert, for first applying the sharkmouth to their Tomahawks in September 1941. Other units took up the marking and soon it was appearing on RCAF, USAAF, RAF and SAAF aircraft in all theatres. The shark mouth continues to be used by many air forces up to the present time.

[Above] Cockpit interior of P-40C showing the instrument panel. [USAF Museum] [Below] Left side of cockpit showing the throttles, trim tab controls, electrical panel, rudder pedal and gas tank switches. [USAF Museum]

[Above] Line up of original AVG pilots in front of the P-40 flown by Robert Smith. The plane sports the "Hell's Angel" insignia of the 3rd Pursuit Squadron and Five victory marks. [USAF Museum] [Below] The first of the AVGs P-40Es sported the teeth and in addition the flying Bengal Tiger insignia plus some rather high code numbers. Individual squadron markings would be added at a later time. Wing roundel was the Chinese rather than American Star. [USAF Museum]

Col. Bruce Holloway and unidentified ground crewman, probably his crew chief, alongside his P-40E of the 23rd Fighter Group, successors to the AVG. Col. Holloway flew with the Flying Tigers and eventually became CO of the Group ending with 13 P-40 kills. [Joe Consiglio]

Line up of 23rd Fighter Group P-40Ns late in the war. The insignia inserted into the sharkmouth is the symbol of the 1st Chinese-American Composite Wing, to which the 23rd now belongs. The second aircraft in the line up is named "Anvil Chorus". First aircraft in line has a tri-color spinner and nose. Note the spiral wheel covers. [H.E. Weichert via Garry Fry]

Kittyhawk Mark I S/N AK86 was assigned to a unit in the Middle East but bears no squadron code nor any other identifying markings. [Mike Garbet]

Flight of Kitthawk Mark Is take off in line abreast formation to reduce amount of dust each had to face. All leading edges of these aircraft were soon scoured down to bare metal and their wind screen and canopies were scored and dulled, hence taking-off with an open canopy was SOP. Sand and grit played havoc with engines and other working parts. [SA War Museum]

Kittyhawk Mark I of No. 2 squadron South African Air Force of Major D.B. Hauptfliesch who was the Commanding officer of the squadron at Amriyha Landing Ground. [SA War Museum]

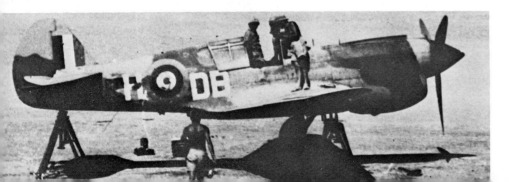

P·40 D-E
Kittyhawk I-IA

The Curtiss H-87A was a substitute for their XP-46 which was dropped because the powers that be decided not to shut down the vital production line to introduce an entirely new airplane. The XP-46 had been conceived as a P-40 Tomahawk replacement, powered by the new Allison V-1710-39 offering more power at altitude. However, the RAF had already placed an order for the Kittyhawk I which was to be powered by the same new Allison engine. The USAAC's Material Division readily concurred with the substitution of an improved P-40 in lieu of the XP-46 and in September, 1940 ordered the British Kittyhawk I as the P-40D.

Curtiss had extensively redesigned the P-40 to improve performance. The fuselage was modified to cut down the cross section area by trimming down the upper section. To improve vision the cockpit enclosure was given new panels. The nose guns were removed and two .50 caliber guns were installed in each wing with provision being made for two 20mm cannon if desired later. The radiator assembly was redesigned, the entire air intake was moved forward to a point just aft of the propeller spinner and deepened. Since the new engine gearing gave a slightly higher line of thrust, the fuselage was shortened by 6 and ¾ inches. The upper air intake was also moved forward to almost touch the spinner; all of these changes altering the shape of the nose. Added fuel capacity was incorporated. Fittings for either a 500 pound bomb or 52 gallon drop tank were provided on the center line of the belly. Pilot armor added up to about 175 pounds on this model. The rounds per gun were now 615 which greatly increased the amount of firepower. The landing gear legs were shortened and the method of retracting the wheels modified.

The Air Corps ordered only 22 P-40Ds while the RAF ordered even less, buying just 20. Serial numbers of the Air Corps batch ran from 40-359, 40-361 through 40-381 while the RAF assigned serials AK571 through AK590 inclusive. The Air Corps cancelled 1,519 of this model later. The P-40D made its first test flight on May 22, 1940. One feature that pleased the combat pilots was the new hydraulic gun chargers. Previously the guns in the wings had been charged by means of a T-handle and cables which worked so poorly that many groups charged the guns on the ground before take off and flew with them "hot".

The Curtiss H-87A-3 was almost identical to the H-87A. Six .50 caliber machine guns were mounted in the wings with around 280 rounds per gun. A flattened type exhaust was introduced midway through the run on this model (the easiest recognition point) and the vertical stabilizer was faired into the fuselage a little better. A few E's were converted into two seaters for training purposes by removing a fuselage tank and installing a second seat but since there didn't seem to be a great need for this type the project was cancelled. Another experiment carried out on an E was the installation of a second set of shackles to permit a pair of 500 pound bombs to be carried in tandem. Ground clearance of the rearward bomb was, at best, marginal. Needless to say this never became popular with pilots and the idea was dropped. Serials for Air Corps versions ran from AC 40-358, 40-382 through 40-681, 41-5305 to 41-5744, and 41-13521 to 41-13599. RAF serials ran from AK 591 through AL 230.

Perfect profile photo of P-40E showing the clean line of the aircraft. [USAF]

[Above Left] Left side of P-40E Cockpit showing flap control, cockpit light, trim tab controls, mixture control, throttle, propellor control fuel selecter, pilot's seat. [Left Below] Right side of cockpit. Items visible include auxiliary hydraulic pump handle, receive control, cabin control unit, identification lights switch box, map case, cowl shutter control lever, rudder pedals. [USAF Museum]

P-40E flown by Col. Holloway of the AVG. Note five victory marks and late style exhaust stubs. S/N 41-5741 indicates that it was one of a block of 440 P-40Es on contract No. AC 15802. [USAF Museum]

P·40D

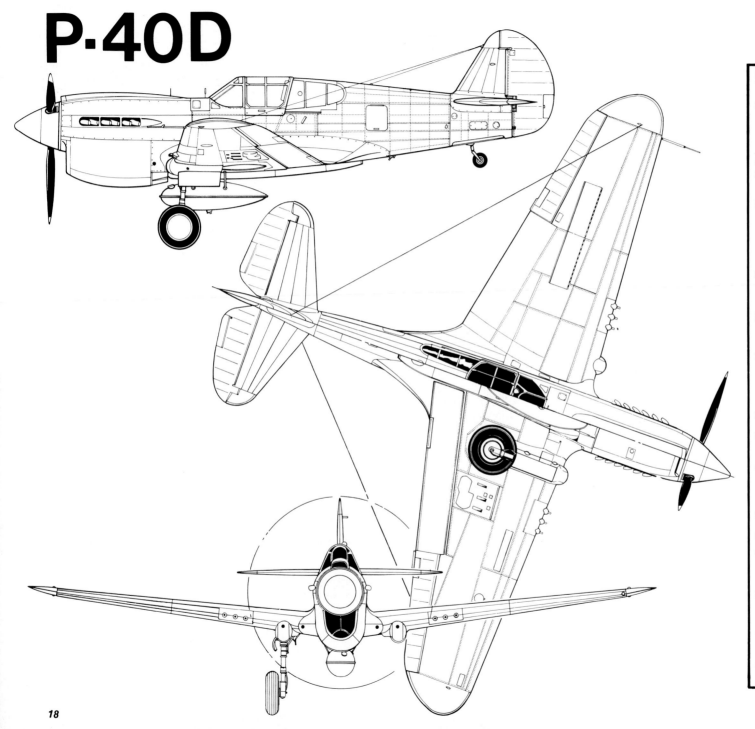

Number of Airplanes	22
Type Supercharger	Engine-driven
	Single stage blower
Dimensions:	
Length	31'8 23/32"
Height	12'4 1/4"
Tread	8' 2 1/8"
Landing Angle	13° 20'
Span	37' 3 1/2"
Weight & Balance:	
Design Gross Wght.	8040
Gross Wght.	8377
Weight Empty	5970
Engine:	
Manufacturer	Allison
Model	V-1710-F3R
Army Designation	V-1710-39
Spec. Numbers	123-D
Take Off Rating	HP 1150
Take Off Rating	RPM 3000-5 min.
Normal Rating	
HP	1000
RPM	2600
Alt.	10,800
Military Rating	
HP	1150
RPM	3000
Alt.	12,000
Propeller:	
Manufacturer	Curtiss
Type	Electric
Diameter	11'0"
Min. Ground	
Clearance	10"
Fuel System:	
No. Fuel Tanks	4
Capacity:	
Normal	120
Maximum	200
Armament:	
Wing Guns - No.,	
Caliber	4, .50
No. Rounds per Gun	615
Gun Sight:	
Location	Top of Inst. Board
Gun Camera:	
Type & Location	H-3, on gun sight
Wing Bombs:	
Quantity & Size	6, 20 lb. M-42 or
	30 lb. M-5 or
	20 lb. T-7
Landing Gear:	
Main Ldg. Tire	
Type	30" S.C., 8 ply
Brake Size	12 x 3 1/4
Radio:	
Type &	
Antenna Type	SCR-283 VEE
Battery:	
Type & Location	G-1, Fuselage

The P-40 Squadron nominated for the title of fighting under the worst conditions has to be the 343-rd Fighter Group's 11th Fighter Squadron in the Aleutians. Sporting a vertical white stripe and a tiger head, it began operations as the 11th Pursuit Squadron in joint operations with 14 Squadron RCAF from April 1942. The "Aleutian Tiger" came into being as a tribute to the father of the Group's CO, the famous Claire Chennault of AVG fame. Blizzards, extreme cold, white-outs, supply problems were everyday occurrences. The planes were specially winterized P-40Es. Note the filled in areas around the exhaust stubs in the photo above. The National insignia is a white star with no surround, a rare variation seen only in the Pacific in 1942. [USAAF and John Moore]

Inlet Development

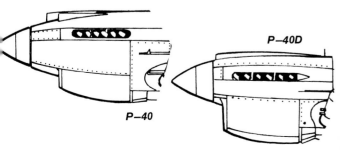

P-40

P-40D

"Texas Longhorn" was flown by First Lt. John D. Landers. A P-40E-1, it was part of the 9th Fighter Squadron, 49th Fighter Group flying from Rorona, New Guinea in 1942. At this stage, Landers had five victories to his credit. A good detail shot of early E style exhaust stubs. [Col. M. Guichet]

[Above Left] P-40Es in a flight shot that was a standard Curtiss publicity photo. The photo was in all probability taken over up-state New York or possibly Canada. It has been credited to at least four different squadrons. One book used it twice listing it first as MK IA Kittyhawks of No. 76 Squadron RAAF and four pages later as Kittyhawks of 112 Squadron RAF. It has also been credited to RAAF No. 75 and RCAF No. 111 Squadrons. [R.C. Jones]

The originators of the sharkmouth theme, No. 112 Squadron RAF had many variations on their aircraft, this one photographed at Sidi Heneish on 4/14/42 is perhaps the most vicious looking of them all. [R.C. Jones]

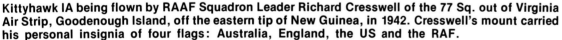

Kittyhawk IA being flown by RAAF Squadron Leader Richard Cresswell of the 77 Sq. out of Virginia Air Strip, Goodenough Island, off the eastern tip of New Guinea, in 1942. Cresswell's mount carried his personal insignia of four flags: Australia, England, the US and the RAF.

[Right Top] Flight Lt. A. Grimmins briefing his 14 Squadron RCAF which flew with the 343rd Fighter Group in the Aleutians. At least one pilot is wearing a USA patch on his shoulder. Note the letter P on the chin and the sharkmouth on this P-40E. The sharkmouth was a tribute to the father of their Group CO, Lt. Col. John Chennault, and a tribute to their American friends. [Canadian Dept. Of National Defense]

[Right] Russian Ace Vicdor Alaghulov sitting on his chute in full uniform studiously persuing a book creating an air of seriousness. [R.C. Jones]

[Right Bottom] The Japanese captured a number of P-40s conveniently crated on the docks of Java. At one time they were contemplating using them in the home defense squadrons but gave up the idea. This example survived the war and was photographed in the area of Atsugi, by James P. Gallagher, 49th Fighter Group.

[Above Left] What the pilot of a P-40F could see while looking through the Mark M-34 gunsight. The air speed indicator is to the left. The X type attachment is the base on which the padding was mounted to cushion the pilot's face and prevent him from hitting the gun sight in a crash. [Above Right] The gunsight with a sun screen in place and the face padding attached to its mount. The instrument panel shows up well in this shot. [Below] Lower half of instrument panel showing rudder controls, various circuit switches and instruction and warning plates. [USAF]

[Below] Actress Elizabeth Bevgner christening the Warhawk "Loyalty", a P-40F-15-CU. The plane carries the name of the group whose war bond purchases paid for it. In the background is Brig. Gen. Willis R. Taylor, CG of Mitchell Field, accepting delivery. This is a middle production F with the flattened exhaust stubs. [John Moore]

LOYALTY
GIFT OF RECENT EMIGRES
FROM NAZI-FASCIST OPPRESSION

P-40F   Kittyhawk II

The Curtiss H-87D was one of the few in the series to go through both the XP and YP development stages. The XP-40F had a British-built Rolls-Royce Merlin engine number 28 with a single-stage, two-speed supercharger to improve altitude performance. Since the Merlin had an updraft carburetor it drew its air through the main air intake at the bottom of the engine cowling. This eliminated the long carburetor air intake atop the cowling and altered the shape of the chin intake slightly. The YP-40F had the Packard-built Merlin V-1650-1. The XP-40F was slightly the faster of the two. The USAAF named the model the Warhawk, a name later applied to the entire series.

The F model, while very similiar to the E model, could now carry a 170 gallon drop tank or a heavier bomb load. Very late in the production run, a radio mast was introduced immediately aft of the cockpit. Early P-40F's had the same 31 feet, 2 inch fuselage as the E but the length of later production airplanes were increased to 33 feet, 4 inches, fin and rudder being moved rearward of the horizontal tail planes. Direction stability, expecially during take-off and landing, was improved by this modification. Don Berlin felt that this was a mistake and that the instability could have been corrected by cutting down the size of the opening of the air scoop. He was certain that the fault was the result of hot air spilling out of the opening and creating turbulence all along the fuselage.

USAAF serials were A.C. 40-326 for the XP-40F, A.C. 41-13602 for the YP-40F, A.C. 41-13600 to 41-13695, 41-13697 to 41-14599 and 41-19733 to 41-20044 for the production run. Although RAF serials FL219 to FL368 were assigned, none of these reached the RAF itself. Some were turned over to the Free French to form the Lafayette Escadrille for service in North Africa, others went on to Russia and a few were returned to the USAAF.

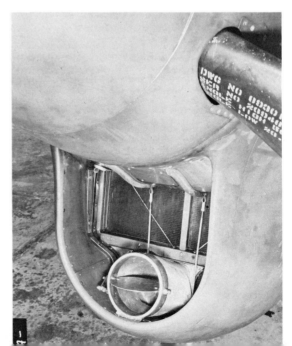

A view down the throat of the revised air scoop of the P-40F. Radiator, oil cooler and carburetor intake have been combined into one intake. [H. Andrews via Gerry Beauchamp]

Inlet Development

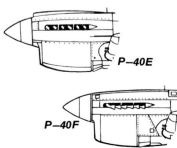

P—40E

P—40F

P·40F

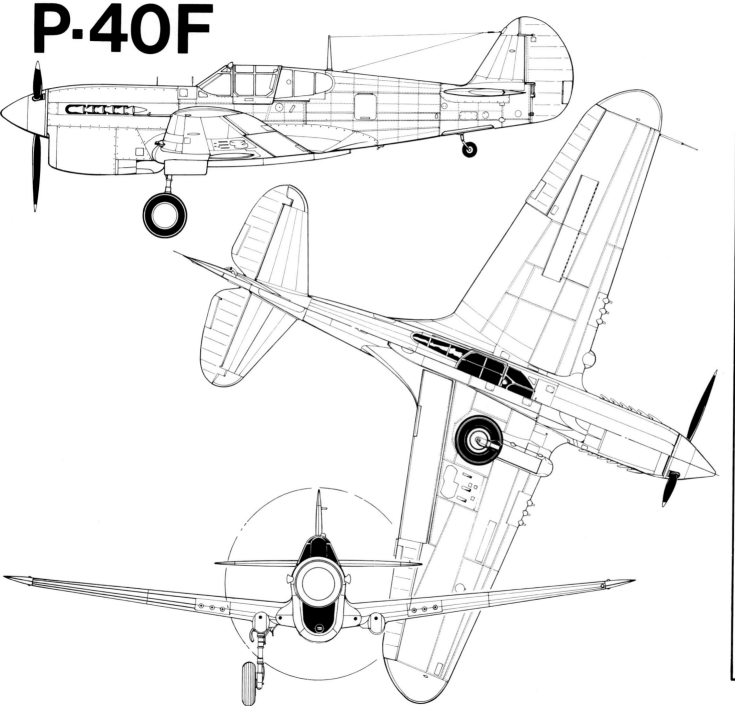

Number of Airplanes	1312
Type Supercharger	Eng. Driven 2-Speed Single stage blower
Dimensions:	
Length	33' 5 23/32"
Height	12' 4 1/4"
Tread	8' 2 1/8"
Landing Angle	13° 10'
Span	37' 3 1/2"
Weight & Balance:	
Design Gross Wght	8368
Gross Wght.	8642
Wght. Empty	6300
Engine:	
Manufacturer	Packard R.R.
Model	Merlin XX
Army Designation	V-1650-1
Spec. Numbers	1025-D
Take Off Rating:	
HP	1300
Take Off Rating:	
RPM	3000
Normal Rating	
HP	995
RPM	2650
Alt.	18,500
Military Rating -	
HP	1105
RPM	2490
Alt.	22,000
Propeller:	
Manufacturer	Curtiss
Type	Electric
Diameter	11' 0"
Minimum Ground	
Clearance	10"
Fuel System:	
No. Fuel Tanks	4 (incl. belly)
Capacity:	
Normal	120
Maximum	200
Armament:	
Wing Guns - No., Caliber	6, .50
No. Rounds per gun	312 #1 Gun 291 #2 Gun 240 #3 Gun
Gun Sight:	
Location	Top of Inst. Board
Gun Camera:	
Type & Location	H-3 on Gun Sight
Wing Bombs:	
Quantity & Size	6, 20 lb. M-42 or 30 lb. M-5 or 20 Lb. T-7
Landing Gear:	
Main Ldg. Tire Type	30" S.C. 8 ply
Brake Size	12 x 3 1/4
Radio:	
Type & Antenna Type	SCR 274-N VEE & MAST
Battery:	
Type & Location	G-1, Fuselage

A shot of Col. Earl E. Bates, 79th Group CO in "Li'l Joe II". The aircraft number was XO*1. Note the lightening flash on the wheel cover and the P-40F of the 79th Group's 87th Fighter Squadron with its "Skeeter" insignia just visible in the background. [R.H. Hoffman]

[Bottom Left] Lt. Col. John Martin, the CO of the 85th Squadron admiring the artistic work of Sgt. Joseph E. Pumphrey who was the great master painter of the Western Desert. Col. Martin lost his life in a post-war accident while flying a P-51 out over the Atlantic as CO of the Virginia ANG. [R.H. Hoffman]

[Bottom Center] Lt. Chuck Bolak poses with his pin-up. Orders were given to remove these beauties when the group left Africa and moved into civilized Italy. [R.H. Hoffman]

[Bottom Right] "Poor Butterfly" catching the attention of Major Joseph W. Connelly of Hartford, Conn. Obviously the Major was an opera lover. [R.H. Hoffman]

Col. Earl E. Bates, 79th Group CO with "Li'l Joe III" and the official insignia of the 79th Fighter Group which was painted on his airplane by the Group Flight Surgeon, Dr. Richards H. Hoffman. The insignia was well thought out and was symbolic of the geographical location of the Group's initiation into Combat, it also served as a memorial to Col. Peter McGoldrick, who was killed while flying with the 57th Group. The Hawk depicted identifies Horus, one of the Egyptian Sun Gods and "Avenger of His Father". The Egyptian characters at the upper right signify the Group number. [R.H. Hoffman, M.D.]

U.S. Army Air Force Serial Number Allocations for Hawk Models H-81 & H-87

Qnty	Model	A.A.F. Serials	C.W. Model
1	XP-40	38-010	Model 81
65	P-40	39-156/220	
68	P-40	39-222/289	
66	P-40	40-292/357	
100	P-40B	41-5205/5304	Model H-81A-2
31	P-40B	41-13297/13327	
193	P-40C	41-13328/13520	Model H-81A-3
1	P-40D	40-159	Model H-87A-2
21	P-40D	40-361/381	
1	P-40E	40-358	Model H-87A-3
300	P-40E	40-382/681	
440	P-40E	41-5305/5744	
79	P-40E	41-13521/13599	
420	P-40E-1-CU	41-24776/25195	
1080	P-40E-1-CU	41-35874/36953	
1	XP-40F	40-360	Model H-87D
96	P-40F	41-13600/13695	
603	P-40F	41-13697/14299	
123	P-40F-5-CU	41-14300/14422	
177	P-40F-10-CU	41-14423/14599	
200	P-40F-15-CU	41-19733/19932	
112	P-40F-20-CU	41-19933/20044	
1	P-40G	39-221	(66th P-40)
600	P-40K-1-CU	42-45722/46321	
200	P-40K-5-CU	42-9730/9929	
335	P-40K-10-CU	42-9930/10264	
165	P-40K-15-CU	42-10265/10429	
50	P-40L-1-CU	42-10430/10479	
220	P-40L-5-CU	42-10480/10699	
148	P-40L-10-CU	42-10700/10847	
112	P-40L-15-CU	42-10848/10959	
170	P-40L-20-CU	42-10960/11129	
60	P-40M-1-CU	43-5403/5462	
260	P-40M-5-CU	43-5463/5722	
280	P-40M-10-CU	43-5723/6002	
400	P-40N-1-CU	42-104429/104828	H-87W
1100	P-40N-5-CU	42-104829/105928	
100	P-40N-10-CU	42-105929/106028	
377	P-40N-15-CU	42-106029/106405	
23	P-40N-20-CU	42-106406/106428	
1500	P-40N-20-CU	43-22752/24251	
319	P-40N-25-CU	43-24252/24570	
180	P-40N-25-CU	43-24572/24751	
500	P-40N-30-CU	44-7001/7500	
500	P-40N-35-CU	44-7501/8000	
220	P-40N-40-CU	44-47749/47968	

P-40A   Model designation only and not assigned.
YP-40F 41-13602 3rd production P-40F with revised cooling system.
P-40H   Model designation only and not assigned.
P-40J   Cancelled P-40E with turbo-supercharger
XP-40K 42-10219 Modified production P-40K-10-CU with wing-root radiators.
P-40P   Designation cancelled
P-40R   300 P-40F & L's with Merlin engines replaced with Allison V-1710-81

P-40F-10-CU of the 69th Fighter Squadron, 57th Fighter Group-the Black Scorpions. This craft, seen in 1943, carries an unusual variety of markings, running the gamut from early RAF style tail flash to Northern Europe-style national insignia.

Richard Lander flew this bombed-up P-40F-20-CU for the 324th Fighter Group also in the Western Desert. This late production F carries a radio mast. As evidence by the underwing bombs, the 324th was primarily used for ground support. [D. Lauder]

Capt. John C.A. Watkins shows the 'roll up your sleeves and get the job done' fashion sported by the Checkertail Clan the 325th Fighter Group in Tunisia. Of special interest is the unusual angular camouflage demarcation of his P-40F. This is a very late production F as noted by the presence of not only the radio mast but also the later P-40 wind screen with extra bracing. [John C.A. Watkins]

[Left Above and Below] Two shots of personal aircraft of the Checkertail's CO, Lt. Col. Robert L. Baseler. After suffering considerable battle damages "stud" was repainted as seen here, Matt Black and Glossy Red, with the distinctive 325th fin, rudder and tail-plane decoration.

Apparently only one P-40G was built, but 50 sets of H81A-2 wings were built and used to convert 44 other P-40 models to the G model. The original G was actually the 66th P-40 A.C. 39-221 which was modified to carry four .30 caliber guns in the wings plus the two .50s in the nose. Additional fuel capacity was provided along with operational armor and self sealing tanks. There were no H, I, or J model designations.

Shots of Sgt. Jean Giscoln and his P-40F-1. Sgt. Giscoln looks as though he is ready for leave in Paris. The stork symbol in front of the canopy represented II Escadrille [SPA 167] while the Sioux head was the "Group Lafayette" marking used by this unit of the Free French Air Force in North Africa. The vertical strips on the rudder are the Blue, White and Red of the Tricolor. [Cdt. Jean Giscoln]

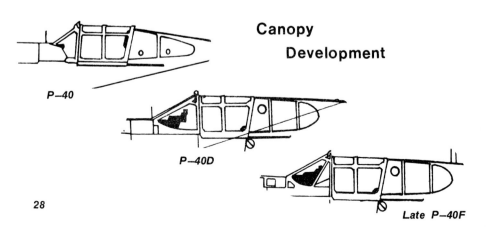

Canopy
Development

P—40

P—40D

Late P—40F

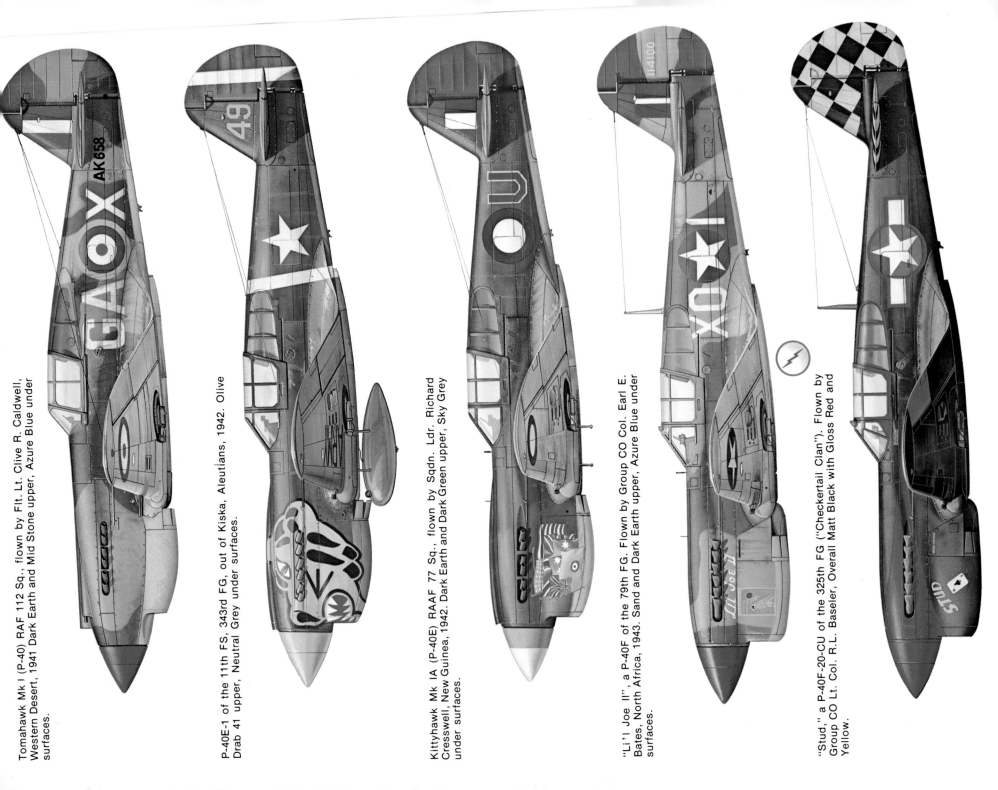

Tomahawk Mk I (P-40) RAF 112 Sq., flown by Flt. Lt. Clive R. Caldwell, Western Desert, 1941 Dark Earth and Mid Stone upper, Azure Blue under surfaces.

P-40E-1 of the 11th FS, 343rd FG, out of Kiska, Aleutians, 1942. Olive Drab 41 upper, Neutral Grey under surfaces.

Kittyhawk Mk IA (P-40E) RAAF 77 Sq., flown by Sqdn. Ldr. Richard Cresswell, New Guinea, 1942. Dark Earth and Dark Green upper, Sky Grey under surfaces.

"Li'l Joe II", a P-40F of the 79th FG. Flown by Group CO Col. Earl E. Bates, North Africa, 1943. Sand and Dark Earth upper, Azure Blue under surfaces.

"Stud," a P-40F-20-CU of the 325th FG ("Checkertail Clan"). Flown by Group CO Lt. Col. R.L. Baseler, Overall Matt Black with Gloss Red and Yellow.

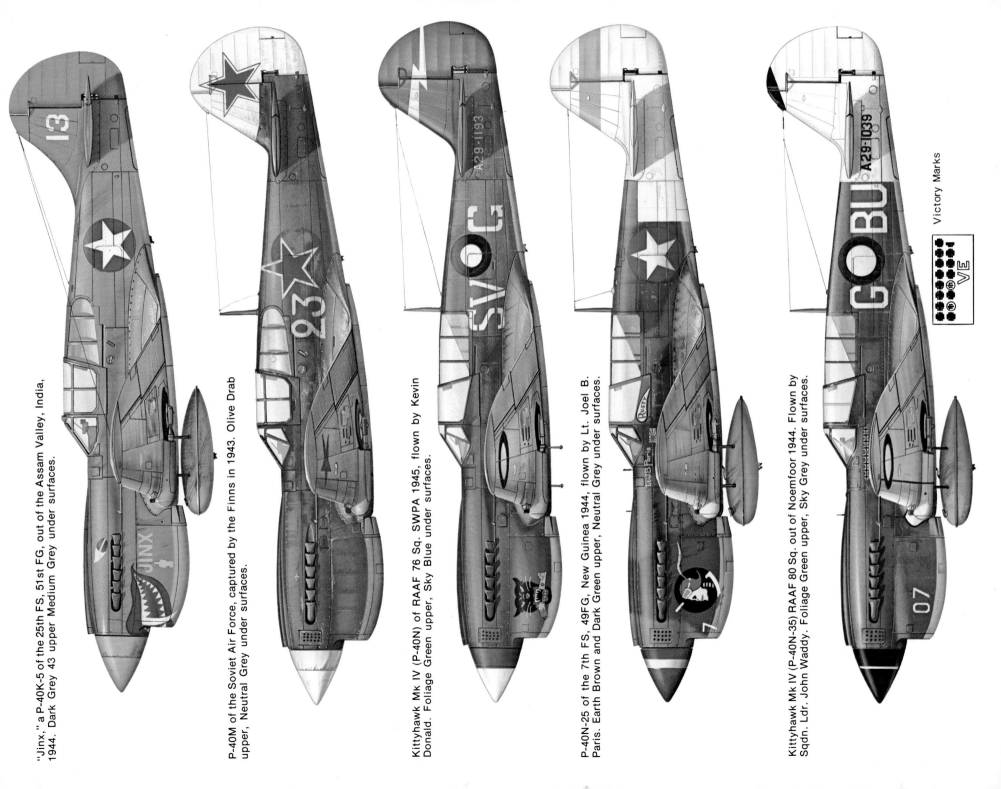

"Jinx," a P-40K-5 of the 25th FS, 51st FG, out of the Assam Valley, India, 1944. Dark Grey 43 upper Medium Grey under surfaces.

P-40M of the Soviet Air Force, captured by the Finns in 1943. Olive Drab upper, Neutral Grey under surfaces.

Kittyhawk Mk IV (P-40N) of RAAF 76 Sq. SWPA 1945, flown by Kevin Donald. Foliage Green upper, Sky Blue under surfaces.

P-40N-25 of the 7th FS, 49FG, New Guinea 1944, flown by Lt. Joel B. Paris. Earth Brown and Dark Green upper, Neutral Grey under surfaces.

Kittyhawk Mk IV (P-40N-35) RAAF 80 Sq. out of Noemfoor 1944. Flown by Sqdn. Ldr. John Waddy. Foliage Green upper, Sky Grey under surfaces.

Victory Marks

The P-40 experienced lateral control problems during its development and this was one attempt to solve the problem by the quick method-adding a dorsal fin. This was an early production P-40F. The solution was obviously insufficient, as later P-40Fs went to the longer fuselage. However, a similar dorsal fin extension was used on early P-40Ks before they, too, were lengthened. [USAF Museum]

A twin-engined P-40 design that at least reached the mock-up stage. The aircraft seems to have been a P-40C S/N 41-13456, but the canopy is of the middle style as introduced on the D, and the engines are F type Merlins. The right side of the right engine nacelle bears a shark-mouth.

The YP-40F was an attempt to streamline the massive and growing intake of the P-40. This was the third production P-40F with the intake moved aft. Whatever the results of this move, it led to no change in the series. [C.W. Photo]

Palm Sunday Massacre

The Palm Sunday Massacre was probably the most successful single engagement for P-40s. Involving all three squadrons of the 57th Fighter Group and 314th Squadron of the 324th Group, as well as 92 Sq. RAF, it took place on Palm Sunday evening, April 18, 1943. Immediately before sundown, P-40s on anti-transport patrol off Cape Bon, Tunisia sighted a huge formation of German aircraft bound for Sicily. Over 60 Ju 52s escorted by 21 fighters were jumped by 46 P-40Fs covered by 11 Spitfires. Caught at low altitude by the Americans diving out of the sun, what followed can only be described as a slaughter. Before the melee ended at dark, 59 Ju 52s and 16 fighters had splashed into the sea or had crash landed on Tunisian soil. Six P-40s failed to return.

One of the victors in the Palm Sunday battle, the 65th Fighter Squadron's Lt. Roy E. Whittaker of Knoxville, Tennessee, downed three Ju-52's in the fray and his crew chief had already painted them on when this photo was taken. Whittaker's rank was still Lieutenant although he had just been promoted to Captain. He ended the War as a Major and scored a total of seven kills with the P-40. [Jackie Spreter]

Armourers loading bombs on an overall Desert Pink and Azure Blue aircraft of the 64th Fighter Squadron's "Black Scorpions". The wheel covers on this P-40F are Blue with a White star. The 64th was a part of the 57th Fighter Group which took part in the Palm Sunday Massacre in which 75 German aircraft were shot down. [USAF]

Kittyhawk Mark III [P-40K] with camouflage scheme applied along with serial number but before national insignia had been added. Note the dorsal fin extension applied to Dash 1 and Dash 5 production. [USAF]

A long fuselaged P-40K-10-CU of the Flying Skulls, the 85th Squadron of the 79th Group in Tunisia in March, 1943. [Dr. R.H. Hoffman]

P-40 K Kittyhawk III

The K model featured a more powerful engine in the Allison V-1710-73 (F4R), otherwise it was a direct continuation of the P-40E. The initial production run had the short E model fuselage which due to the additional power had a tendency to swing during take-off. In the K-1 through the K-5 batches, an extended dorsal fin was added to correct this problem. Batches K-10 to K-15 changed over to the longer P-40F fuselage. The later K marks could be distinguished by the E type nose with its separate carburetor inlet and the lack of radio mast introduced on the F model combined with the long fuselage. The K had an automatic manifold pressure altitude regulator. The British term for this feature was automatic boost control. The P-40K-5 had rotary valve cooling added. Some of the aircraft from these batches destined for Alaska and the Aleutians were winterized. The K had been intended to be sent to China. The K also introduce a new strengthened forward canopy. In another of the unaccountable moves so far as designations are concerned, Curtiss took a P-40K-10 airframe and gave it the XP-40K designation. It was modified to test fly the V-1650-1 Allison Merlin engine and also the radiator in the wing concept.

Air Force serials were A.C. 42-9730 to 42-10429 and 42-45722 to 42-46321. The RAF took 21 K's as Kittyhawks Mark IIIs serialled from FL710 to FL730.

The P-60A was then to have replaced the P-40 on the production line but problems with the new plane caused the Air Force to increase their order for the P-40K.

A P-40 seaplane? Just a P-40K of the 343rd Group's 18th Squadron that came down in the middle of a small Alaskan Lake. [USAF]

Tail Development

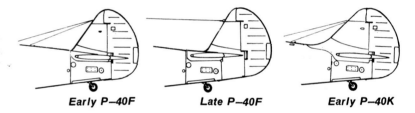

Early P—40F   Late P—40F   Early P—40K

It was a tough life for the P-40Ks in the far North. This one was handled a bit rough by a pilot of the 18th Squadron, 343rd Fighter Group.

You could twist a P-40K-1 and partially crush it as Lt. Milt Cunningham of the 343rd Squadron did after aborting a take-off at 100 feet. His engine failed on take off and he attempted to land on one of the other runways. The plane cartwheeled but Cunningham like so many other Warhawk pilots walked away. [N. Taylor]

"Jinx" and "Liz" of the 51st Fighter Group flying out of the Assam Valley in the CBI went the others one better and created a saber-toothed shark-mouth. But instead of a mean look, it gives the impression that they have dined well. [USAF]

Exhaust Development

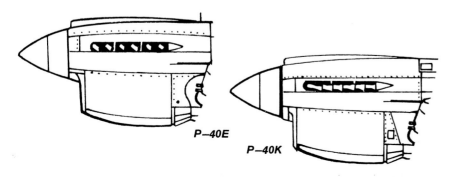

P—40E

P—40K

Officials of the Buffalo, New York plant took over "Susie Q" which had been modified to include twin cockpits, dual controls and a tricycle landing gear to train ground crew mechanics how to taxi and move an aircraft under its own power from one location to another. This P-40K had been rendered unflyable. [USAF]

While Curtiss never produced a P-40J the designation was to have applied to a P-40E which was to have been fitted with a new turbo unit. Two seat training versions were referred to as TP-40s. RP-40s and ZRP-40s were designations assigned to denote that the aircraft were restricted in use and/or obsolete as the term applied. A few other odd P-40s popped up from time to time, some were rebuilt in combat theaters of parts of several different P-40 models. One had the moniker "Bitsahawk" applied by the unit that produced it. There was a trainer version with a third wheel hung under the nose to produce a tricycle gear type aircraft (shown above) and another P-40 sported a tracked landing gear in lieu of the conventional wheels. This one was to have been used on rough terrain, it was tested but never used in the field. About the only thing not done to a P-40 was to hang a hook on it under the tail and try to sell it to the Navy as a carrier fighter.

Parallel Developments

The P-40, always adequate, was also always a step behind its competition and enemies, particularly in altitude performance. Development was continuous in an effort to produce its successor. Yet each, as it was designed and tested, proved to possess too small a margin of improvement to merit interruption of assembly lines.

The XP-46 was an attempt to up-power and clean up the P-40C, introducing the more robust Allison V-1710-39. Intended to give a maximum speed of 410 mph at 15,000 feet, it in fact produced only 355 mph and was dropped for the similarly powered P-40D.

The XP-53 was to have combined N.A.C.A.'s laminar-flow airfoil and the then under-development Continental 1,600 hp XIV-1430-3 inverted vee with the basic P-40 airframe. Two prototypes were ordered but neither flew as an XP-53. The second was re-engined and redesignated the XP-60, the first sacrificed armor, self-sealing tanks and armament to the second and ended its life ingloriously as a static test airframe for the XP-60 series, never flying at all.

The XP-60 series resulted from the fact that deliveries of the Continental engine intended for the XP-53 were doubtful at best. The Army Air Corps therefore requested that the second XP-53 prototype be fitted with the British-built Merlin 28. Lacking even the basic rudiments of a combat aircraft, the aircraft, now called the XP-60, flew on September 18, 1941. But choice of the Merlin to power other U.S. fighters, such as the P-51, led to a frantic scramble to find a replacement.

Before the process was complete, no less than four other engines were intended for or fitted into the airframe: the Allison V-1710-75 at 1,425 hp (one actually built as the XP-60A), the same engine with different supercharger (one built as the XP-60B), the Chrysler XIV-2220 (intended to be the XP-60c but never completed as such), the Merlin 61 (XP-60D), and the P+W R-2800 radial installed with a four-bladed airscrew in the XP-60B airframe (redesignated XP-60E) and finally with six-bladed contra-rotating props in the half-finished XP-60C (retaining that designation). By this time, with new wings, modified tail surfaces, revised canopy and a radial engine, the XP-60E bore no external resemblance at all to its parent, the P-40.

One YP-60E was produced in 1944, but showed no promise of improving on planes already on assembly lines. Never put into production, it marked the end of P-40 lineage. The P-40 line, it seems, had come full circle, born a radial-engined pursuit plane as the P-36, it faded as a radial-engined interceptor.

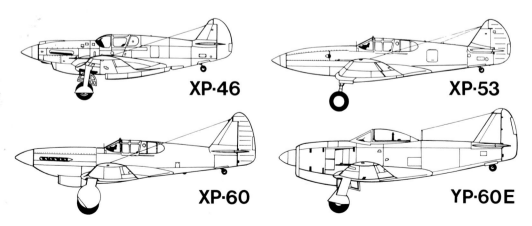

XP-46   XP-53

XP-60   YP-60E

[Above] Curitss XP-60 was an improved version of the P-40 which incorporated the best design features of the XP-53. The XP-53 in turn was to have been a successor to P-40. To complicate matters further the XP-60 was reconfigured into the XP-60D. [Above Right] [USAF Museum]

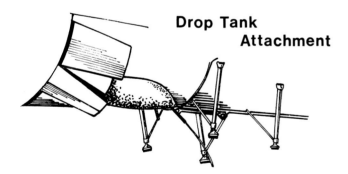

Drop Tank Attachment

Another attempt at improving the strain, the XP-40K S/N 42-10219 was used to test a new radiator arrangement. The radiators were located in the center section of the wing, which had been thickened for this purpose. A concept that would be turned to later in the XP-40Q. [CW Photo]

P-40 L
Kittyhawk II

In an effort to gain improved performance, the L was lightened in every way possible without a major redesign. All but the first L's had two wing guns. Armor, fuel capacity, and other items reduced or omitted and a weight savings of about 450 pounds was achieved. For all this, the increase in speed was just 4 mph and many of the changes were later reworked in the field adding probably 200 of the 450 pound saving back onto the aircraft. A radio mast was installed just aft of the cockpit making the L easy to distinguish from all but the last F's. The L-1 had the short fuselage while the others had the longer version. Otherwise the P-40L was pretty much externally identical to the later long-fuselage F. both marks being powered by the Allison-built Merlin. The number of wing guns was a more reliable distinction.

Some wag tagged the L model "the Gypsy Rose Lee." As Miss Lee was the foremost strip-tease artiste of the day, the name sort of fit. The RAF added to the confusion by naming it the Kittyhawk Mark II, a designation they had already given the P-40F. USAAF Serials ran from A/C 42-10430 through 42-11129. On the P-40L-5 rocket fittings were added to the wings. The Dash 10 had the armor removed from the coolant tank, some warning lights were taken off the panels, the auxiliary fuel pump was moved and sway braces were added to the belly tank. The Dash 15 had an interior aircraft signal light added and a permanent type of carburetor filter. The Dash 20 was given an SCR-695 radio, an incendiary grenade installation, and improved relays.

While some skull insignias were purely personal markings others were used by entire squadrons. The 85th Fighter Squadron of the 79th Fighter Group were known as the "Flying Skulls" not only did the winged skull grace the cowls of their P-40 but also their flight jackets. Major Fred Schoellkopf is sporting one on his. [Dr. R.H. Hoffman]

[Below left] Another shot of the "Flying Skulls" shows the bleakness of the terrain in the Western Desert. Note the exhaust outlets of the parked plane are canvas covered to protect them from sand.

This P-40 1-CU of the 86th Fighter Squadron, 79th Fighter Group in North Africa. "Punchy II" was flown by Flight Officer Vincent Walls. [W. West]

P-40L-1-CU of the all-black 99th Fighter Squadron of the 332nd Fighter Group. These were the lightweights of the series. Note the RAF style tail flash. [Dr. R.H. Hoffman]

Landing Gear

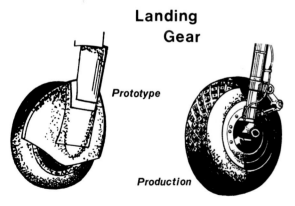

Prototype

Production

"Mona II" a P-40L-10-CU which was flown by a black pilot of the 99th Fighter Squadron. The terrain was suited for this sort of landing which undoubtedly saved a lot of lives. [Dr. R.H. Hoffman]

P-40L-5-CU A/S/N 42-10664 Aircraft No. 44 belonged to the Commanding Officer, Lt. Col. Gordon H. Austin, of the 325th Fighter Group, The Checkertail Clan. "Lighthouse Louie" is pictured in Tunisia, North Africa in 1943. [CT Clan]

[Above Left] Number 40 "Trixie" was the P-40 flown by Capt. Joe Bloomer of the 318th and the interesting item on his aircraft is the belly tank which the pilots and ground crew made into a bomb of sorts by adding a fin and a fuse made from a hand grenade and detonator. The idea was to drop the tank when it was low on fuel on some target of opportunity and hopefully set fire to it. It did meet with some success but was abandoned for safety reasons. The nose insignia is "Trixie" leading a Green dragon on a chain. The Green dragon was the 318th Squadron's insignia and name.

Unnumbered 325th Fighter Group P-40 which crash landed at Mateur, Tunisia following a mid-air collision on the 3rd of July 1943. The group was strafing a radar installation at Pula, Sardinia when the two P-40s collided. The pilot of the other P-40, Lt. Bryant was killed when his tailless plane dove into the ground. [John C.A. Watkins]

P-40M-1 of the 44th Fighter Squadron on Munda Field, New Georgia, Solomon Islands in August of 1943. The 18th Fighter Group arrived just as soon as the area was secure and went into action promptly. Note Pacific style national insignia without Yellow surround and the White stripe under the wing. [USAF]

P-40M
Kittyhawk III

The P-40M was similiar to the K series. Originally it was intended solely for the RAF. An Allison V-1710-81 engine replaced the Merlin. A perforated cooling grill was added just forward of the exhaust stubs and a set of reinforced ailerons were installed. The M was a long fuselage aircraft distinguishable from the K by virtue of the radio mast. Three .50 machine guns were carried in each wing. The Dash 5 had the permanent carb air filter. The Dash 10 differed from the others by having an air vapor eliminator, fuel pressure warning signal, and a visual landing gear indicator installed on the upper surface of each wing like the Focke-Wulf 190. These were colored pins that protruded above the surface when the gear was extended. They replaced the warning horn system used on prior P-40s.

The RAF designated these as Kittyhawk IIIs like the P-40K from which it was derived. Serials ran from FL-875 to FL-905, FR-111, to FR-140, FR-210 to FR-361, FR-383 to FR-392, FR-414 to FR-521, FR-779 to FR-872 and FS-100 to FS-268 all numbers inclusive. All but five of the six hundred built were sent to the RAF but, according to one source, for some reason the USAAF assigned serials A/C 43-5403 to 43-6002 to the series.

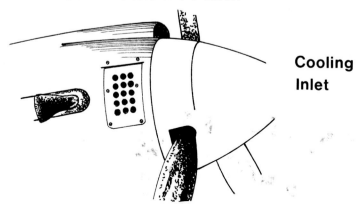

Cooling Inlet

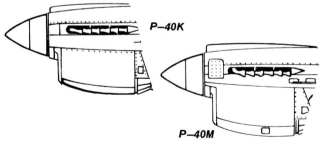

An RAF P-40M, unit unknown, bearing the name "Gasport, N.Y." and a serial number 850 appears to have had the fuselage and wing national insignias over painted. [E. Nicolle]

Nose Development

P-40M of the 23rd or 51st Fighter Group, based in India in 1943. The 51st carried the same sharkmouth as the 23rd Fighter Group, and operated with it in India and then China. Only the presence of three wing guns distinguished this from an N-1. [Garry L. Fry]

The P-40N-30-CU flown by Major Ben Preston C.O. of the 13th Pursuit Group was natural metal aircraft trimmed in Black and Orange. Preston as a Colonel would later lead the 4th Fighter Group in the Korean War and become a Mig killer. [USAF]

A P-40N-1 could easily have been mistaken for a P-40M if the serial number was not known. This P-40N-1 was one that did not have the rear decking cut out and the new modified canopy. [USAF Museum]

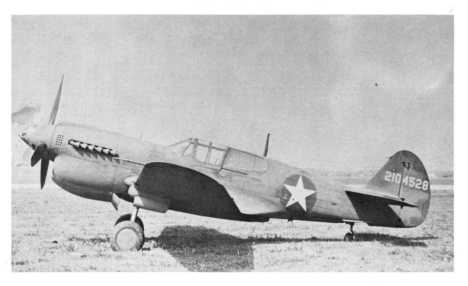

P-40 N Kittyhawk IV

Curtiss assigned model number H-87W to the N series. This was the last major production model of the series. It was the fastest Warhawk at 378 mph. In what amounted to a last effort, Curtiss made a number of modifications all designed to improve the breed. Every effort was made to lighten the plane. The front wing tank was removed. Two machine guns were eliminated. Smaller lighter wheels were substituted and aluminum oil coolers and radiators replaced the old heavy brass ones. Head armor was introduced. A V-1710-81 engine with automatic boost control provided the power. To improve pilot rear vision a modification was made to the canopy giving it a frameless sliding hood and the rear deck was cut out deeper while the aft portion of the canopy was squared off. This was the primary external distinction of the Mark on all except the earliest N's. About half way through the run, the forward canopy was simplified by the removal of some bracing struts.

The Dash 5 model received a new SCR-696 radio, a new pilot's seat, and recognition lights. The external bomb racks and drop tank fittings were put back on this model. The Dash 10 lost two of the wing guns but added a new rate of climb and manual oil dilution system and other cold weather operation items. The Dash 15 regained the two machine guns and the larger wing tank. The Dash 20 was given fittings to carry three 500 pound bombs. The Dash 25 was fitted with non-metal self sealing gas tanks and some other minor changes were made. The Dash 30 had a few minor equipment changes internally. The Dash 35 had some minor instrument changes made to it and was given a new radio and ADF system. The Dash 40 was the last of the Ns. It was fitted with automatic boost and propeller control, a new oxygen system, flame supressing exhaust stacks and the armor was relocated. The N was the most numerous of the series and the best all around aircraft. A total of 5,219 were built, and the last S.N. 44-47964 rolled out on November 30, 1944. There was no P-40P as the designation was reassigned to a block of the N series.

P-40N

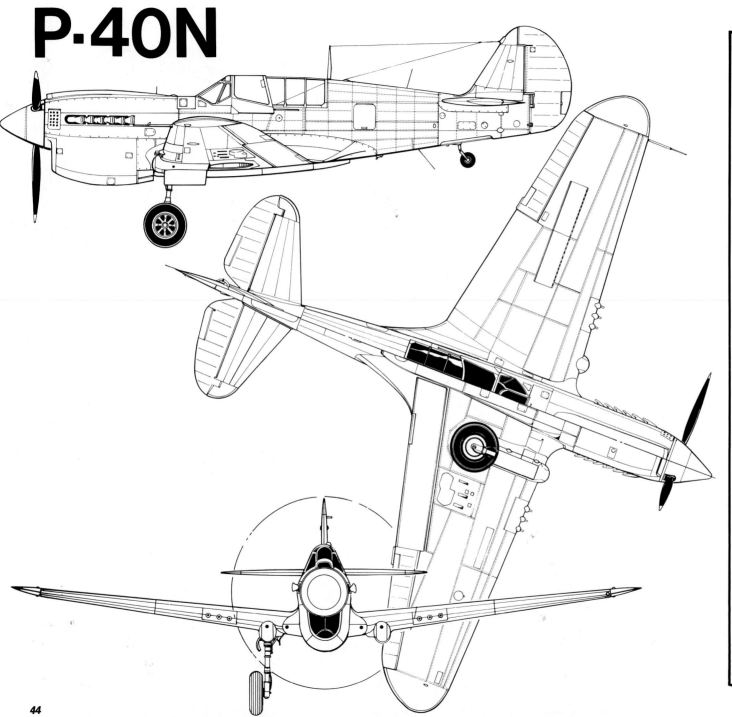

Number of Airplanes	2000
Type Supercharger	Eng. Driven
	Single stage blower
Dimensions:	
Length	33' 5 23/32"
Height	12' 4 1/2"
Tread	8' 2 1/2"
Landing Angle	13° 5'
Span	37' 3 1/2"
Weight & Balance:	
Design Gross Wght.	
Gross Wght.	8350
Wght. Empty	6200
Engine:	
Manufacturer	Allison
Model	V-1710-F20R
Army Designation	V-1710-81
Spec. Numbers	163-A
Take Off Rating:	
HP	1200
Take Off Rating:	
RPM	2800-5 min.
Normal Rating	
HP	1000
RPM	2600
Alt.	14,000
Military Rating -	
HP	1125 B.H.P.
RPM	3000
Alt.	15,500
Propeller:	
Manufacturer	Curtiss
Type	Electric
Diameter	11' 0"
Min. Ground	
Clearance	10"
Fuel System:	
No. Fuel Tanks	3 (incl. belly)
Capacity:	
Normal	120
Maximum	210
Armament:	
Wing Guns - No.,	
Caliber	4 (place for 6), .50
No. Rounds per Gun	312 #1 Gun
	291 #2 Gun
	240 (provision only)
Gun Sight:	
Location	Top of Inst. Board
Gun Camera:	
Type & Location	L.G. Fairing (R.H.)
Wing Bombs:	
Quantity & Size	None
Landing Gear:	
Main Ldg. Tire	
Type	27" S.C. 8 ply rated
Brake Size	11 x 3
Radio:	
Type &	SCR 522 or 274
Antenna Type	Mast (Type AN-74)
Battery:	
Type & Location	AN-W-B-149,
	Fuselage

P-40N-10-CU of the 18th Fighter Squadron, 343rd Fighter Group in the Aleutians, spiral on spinner and wheels were Blue and Orange. Petty girl was a blonde in a pale blue suit with flesh tones where appropriate. This was a winterized version with a manual oil dilution system and only two guns per wing. [Henry Leslie]

[Above Right] It is very doubtful that the Walt Disney Studio would have given official approval to the insignia sported on this P-40 of the 18th Squadron based in the Aleutians. The Blue Foxes expressed their personal feeling for the enemy in this insignia.

The other extreme of climate. A tarp over the cockpit area keeps it from becoming too hot for comfort. A home made work bench for the armorer provided a better than average work area. This P-40N of the 15th Group's 45th Squadron on Nanumes Island is being readied for a mission by its armorers. [USAF]

P-40N-15-CU of the 7th Fighter Squadron, 49th Fighter Squadron at Biak in September 1944. The 49th produced possibly the greatest variety of markings worn by the P-40, sharing only a white tail and wing leading edge in common. And these were frequently altered by personal variations. [James P. Gallagher]

Lt. Miller flew this P-40 with a diamond checkered rudder, number 16 of the 7th Squadron. A Zero chased him 50 miles before forcing him to crash land. [Bob Kopitzke]

The unnumbered P-40 with the checkered rudder was the aircraft of Capt. Richard Vodra, an ace with the 49th Fighter Groups 8th Squadron. Dick is the middle man in the photo. His aircraft number was 57 and later bore the number and the nickname of Squirrel Bait. Another 49er, Lt. Danny Moore, also flew a similiar marked P-40 with checker rudder. It was a personal joke between himself and Joe Littleton. Both were from Louisiana and as Joe got shot up pretty roughly by "Wewak Willie" or "Sakie of Wewak" a colorful Zero pilot who flew a Zero that was completely checked overall, Danny painted his rudder as a challenge to the Checkered Zero to come up and fight so he could defend the honor of Louisiana.

[Above Right] Capt. Dick Vodra, wears the over water dress favored by the fashion-conscious pilots of the SWPA. The Mae West was a must. Modelers note the ragged lines of the rudder checks and take heart. [R. Vodra]

49th Fighter Group pilot using the skull as a personal insignia was Capt. Joel B. Paris who flew among other P-40's, the P-40N-25 illustrated in color. Paris finished the war with nine victories.

A rarity, a natural metal P-40. This particular bird is a P-40N-25 of the 7th Squadron, 49th Fighter Group photographed at Middleburg Island after a sweep over Sorong and other western points of Dutch New Guinea. At the time the 7th was at Biak Island getting ready to convert to the P-38. Note remnant aircraft serial number under the tail plane, mostly covered by the national insignia and the 49th's distinctive white tail.

The 80th Fighter Group which was made up of the 88th, 89th, 90th and 459th Squadrons was assigned to the 10th Air Force in the CBI theater of the operations. Operating out of Upper Assam Valley, India from their base at Naggaghuli they flew ground support missions for the Allied drives in Northern Burma. The group's P-40s were certainly among the most colorful P-40Ns of the entire War. Each had a skull painted on both sides of the cowl and no two were alike. Photos reveal that numbers ranged from 12 up to 62, also that spinners were of several different shades or colors, Numbers 12, 15, and 35 had light spinners, Number 49 had a very dark spinner and others in the 40-50-60 series had dark spinners. It is possible that these were Red, Yellow, and Blue as these were used most frequently to designate squadrons by colors.

"Joanne" number 49 is an interesting shot. Note the drop tank is on backwards. The spinner is extremely dark, so much so that it appears to be Black, but is probably Blue. The wheel cover sports a pair of dice. The spots read 4 and 3 for usual 7. [Bob Gebhardt]

The photo above is unusual in that only the jaw bones and teeth show, possibly the upper cowl was damaged and replaced and an eye hastily painted in or that portion of the cowl could have come from a hanger queen that had the sharkmouth scheme. Note also that this aircraft has three drop tanks mounted possibly for ferrying or photo recon work.

Canopy Development

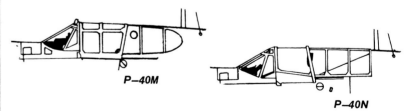

P–40M

P–40N

[Left Above & Left] Red-nosed P-40Ns of the 80th Group. Cleaned up and lined up, they are probably awaiting an inspection.

If the Flying Tigers were the best of the P-40 Groups of the entire war, No. 75 Squadron of the RAAF has to be ranked as one of the best individual squadrons. While the AVG was made up of crack pilots with plenty of experience, 75 was hastily thrown together with untrained and inexperienced pilots and thrust into the breech in New Guinea against superior Japanese pilots and planes. Despite being almost wiped out, they held their ground and wrote a special chapter in aerial history. Late in the War, 10 July 1945 their P-40Ns on Tarakan Island looked really sharp, a far cry from the rag tag days early in the war. [Eric Nicolle]

Standing a Kittyhawk on its nose took a minimum of effort, but getting it down called for a maximum effort as these members of No. 75 Squadron of the RAAF demonstrate. The strip at Tarakan was turned into a mudhole by rains in June of 1945 and this was just one of a number of accidents. [Dave Weatherill]

A line up of Kittyhawk IVs of 76 Squadron RAAF. Planes are overall RAF Dark Green [called Foliage Green by the Aussies] with Sky Blue under surfaces.

Squadron Leader John Waddy standing by his P-40N-20 or Kittyhawk Mark IV. Coded G-BU serial number A29-607. The plane had the Black spinner and White tail of No. 80 Squadron RAAF. Waddy had 15½ P-40 kills. He flew several different P-40s with this squadron and each of them had serial numbers that totaled up to 13, if one ignores the A-29 prefix, 6 + 7 = 13. The "VE" under the canopy refers to Waddy's part in the victory in Europe. He first achieved fame flying with 112 Sq. RAF in the Western Desert. [Eric Nicole]

[Below Left] A little later shot of Waddy's plane and the rest of 80 Squadron RAAF being bombed up at Noemfoor, 1944. The white tails now have a Black tip to reflect spinner color, and "07" in the foreground has a White band on its spinner indicating it belongs to the CO.

Number 82 Squadron of the RAAF used a Red and White checkered band across the fin and rudder of their P-40Ns.

A P-40N [Kittyhawk IV] of No. 450 Squadron RAAF Coded OK-D S/N FR853 photographed in Italy. This photo gives an excellent view of the engine, its mountings and the radiators as well as the interior of the cowling. It also illustrates the primative equipment that the ground crews had to rely on to get the job done, one mechanic is standing on an oil drum to reach the area he is working on. The Australian make-up of the Squadron couldn't possibly be mistaken after viewing the personal marking on the cowling.   [G.H. Brian via Mike Garbett]

[Above Right] The RAAF pilots of the 450 Squadron in Italy were a dashing lot and favored the short sleeve shirt along with shorts. The casual look was the in thing among these Kittyhawk IV chaps. A kangaroo kicking a dachshund is the cowling insignia.

A minimum effort could be expended when the proper equipment was at hand, getting the aircraft off the ground after it had flipped over was no problem but getting it right side up was a different story. This Army Salvage Unit vehicle has taken a Kittyhawk IV of No. 450 Squadron in charge somewhere in Italy in 1944. A man on each wing tip for balance and a couple with a set of the portable wheels at the tail and away we go! The AOK code wasn't an apt one. [M. Garbett]

Number 120 Squadron [later No. 120 Sqdn. Militaire Luchtvaart] of the Royal Netherlands East Indies Army operated with the RAAF. Dutch serial numbers beginning with C3 were assigned to fighters. The C3-526 was in light blue. Insignia was carried in the usual six positions. It was in the form of the Dutch flag. Later the Dutch flew P-40Ns in bare metal finish with the Dutch tricolor roundel with small orange center. The RNEIA was the last outfit to fly the P-40 in actual combat, using them against the Rebels in 1948 in the NEI. [G.H. Kamphuis via G.J. Zwanenburg]

[Below Left] The Chinese Nationalist was another nation that used the P-40N during the immediate post war period. This specimen was photographed at Kangwan Air Force Base in 1946. [Earl Reinert Collection]

The last of the line, P-40N-40-CU Serial Number 44-47968. Decked with dollars and flags, crepe paper as streamers and a sign reading "News Smokes for Soldiers" and a shamrock just forward of the cockpit, the last of the series sits in the final assembly area. [USAF Museum]

[Above Right] TP-40N-30-CU, Warhawk that was converted to a two seater. The dash 30 was built in quantity as 500 were produced but only a few were re-made into tandem jobs. This two place TP-40 was a training aircraft and was used to give transitional training to advanced single engine Cadet trainees or to newly commissioned fighter pilots before sending them up alone in an actual fighter. [USAF Museum]

[Far Right] TP-40N-35-CU, S/N 447541 was another one of those converted to a two seater.

Final Modifications

A single P-40N fuselage was modified, as the XP-40N, to improve further all-round vision. In the same fashion as the P-47 and P-51, the rear spine was cut down and the original canopy replaced by a blown bubble hood. This, however, remained a solitary prototype, dropped in favor of the XP-40Q in a final attempt to continue the P-40 series.

There was only a single example built as the XP-40Q, but it appeared in three distinct forms. In its original form, it was an almost exact duplicate of the XP-40K, testing the same radiator placement, in a swollen wing center-section. The resemblance wasn't accidental as both planes were developed off production K airframes. The difference was that the XP-40Q mounted the 1,425 hp Allison V-1710-121 engine in the place of the standard engine, and drove a four-bladed propeller.

After a period of testing, the Q was taken in hand for further modification, aimed at greater increases in performance. It emerged looking like a slimmed-down XP-40N. Like its predecessor it had the cut-down rear fuselage and bubble hood, but had a much shallower chin scoop. The third modification clipped the wing-tips, reducing the span by over two feet.

It was the fastest of the P-40 series with a top speed of 422 mph at 20,000 ft. But for all this effort, since the Q was still inferior to Thunderbolts and Mustangs then in production further development was abandoned. P-40R was the final designation in the series. It did not represent any new attempt or major change in the series. It simply consisted of some 300 odd P-40Fs and P-40Ls that had their Packard-built Merlins replaced by Allisons. This change was necessitated by a shortage of the Merlins.

[Top] Close up of the XP-40N showing the bubble canopy in the open position. Note that the National insignia has a Red surround. [USAF Museum]

[Center] The XP-40Q in its original form.

[Bottom] XP-40Q second form with wing guns mounted. Note the underwing pilot tube, a departure from the Curtiss practice. [USAF Museum]

Two famous Curtiss Wright aircraft, the XP-40Q and C-46 Commando. [USAF Museum]

The end of the line. The XP-40Q-1 in civilian racing colors. In an odd incident at the 1947 Thompson Throphy races pilot Joe Ziegler had not qualified but flew the aircraft anyway. The engine quit on the 13th lap and Joe bailed out ending the flying career of the Q. [Earl Reinert]

More US Fighters of World War Two

1036 F6F Hellcat

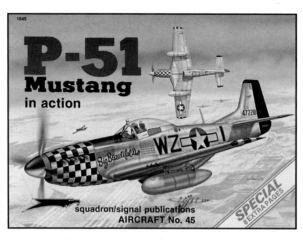

1045 P-51 Mustang

1067 P-47 Thunderbolt

1081 F2A Buffalo

1106 P-61 Black Widow

1145 F4U Corsair

from squadron/signal publications